T0147246

Watering Harvest

The Treasure He Is

Susie Michaels

WESTBOW®
PRESS
A DIVISION OF THOMAS NELSON
& ZONDERVAN

Edited by: Rev. Charles Fritts

Scripture quotations are from:
The Holy Bible, New King James Version (NKJV)
@ 1984 by Thomas Nelson, Inc.

WestBow Press books may be ordered through booksellers or by contacting:

WestBow Press
A Division of Thomas Nelson & Zondervan
1663 Liberty Drive
Bloomington, IN 47403
www.westbowpress.com
1 (866) 928-1240

ISBN: 978-1-4908-4199-1 (sc)
ISBN: 978-1-4908-4200-4 (hc)
ISBN: 978-1-4908-4201-1 (e)

Library of Congress Control Number: 2014911287

Printed in the United States of America.
WestBow Press rev. date: 07/16/2014

This book is dedicated to the Father, the Son,
and the Holy Spirit,
with humility I stand in awe of You.

Contents

Acknowledgments

To my husband who loves me and graciously supported me during the writing of this book. God gave me you, because He knew you. For that I am thankful.

In memory of my loving mother and father. You planted that I might water, trusting God to give the increase.

Preface

DEAR Reader,

It is my prayer that as you read *Watering Harvest* you will receive the friendly words of the characters as refreshing words of life; nourishing you with the good news of who God Is.

And as the characters testify of the Treasure living within them, I pray you will discover the significance God has placed within you. As He has also chosen you to cherish and share the Treasure He Is.

Surely you, are the apple of God's eye, the harvest of His heart,

Susie Michaels

King Solomon filled the temple of God
with priceless treasure.
King Jesus paid the price of His life to fill us
with The Treasure He Is.

Outer Court

Hope

DOLPHINS dove and splashed near the boat, causing quite a stir as Vessel and Harvest fished the waters of the Avowal River.

The local fishermen's report claimed redfish had been running the river all week. The men hoped today would be the day both of them would reel in a big redfish.

By midmorning, though, they had caught nothing about which to boast; and their prospect of catching the big redfish was fading fast. Nevertheless, Vessel remained hopeful, enjoying every cast of his line. After all, it was a beautiful, warm December day. The sky was sunny and blue; and with the exception of splashing dolphins, there was complete peace on the face of the water.

Harvest, on the other hand, could have cared less how perfect the day was. He was on the water solely to catch fish, and today he wanted to catch a big redfish. So far, he had caught nothing with the exception of two baby trout and a puffer fish, and those three had taken up his good bait. As each minute passed, Harvest felt growing frustration. To make matters worse, Vessel insisted on whistling a carefree tune, as if he were actually enjoying watching the dolphin's splash, knowing their useless antics were scaring off all the good fish.

Harvest burst out, "How do you do that? How can you not care we've been fishing all morning but caught nothing? Then you whistle as if the dolphins need your help scaring all the good fish away. Why do you not get angry or frustrated like a normal person?"

Vessel laughed and said, "I imagine I just don't have it in me."

Harvest shot him a questioning look as he reeled in his fishing line only to find, once again, an empty hook.

Vessel shrugged. "What can I say? All of my space is occupied, leaving no room to harbor the anger or frustration of your so-called 'normal person.'"

Harvest just shook his head. "You've got to be the oddest friend I have ever had. Who doesn't have space available? What does that even mean?"

Vessel smiled and simply restated what he had said. "My life is full. All of the space within me has been taken."

"Well, I would like to know how you keep your space so full," Harvest said, "since I always seem to have more than enough space in my life to harbor anger and frustration."

"It's simple. The space within my life is eternally filled with Treasure," Vessel declared. Harvest stared at his friend curiously, his forehead creased and his eyebrows scrunched.

Vessel, seeing his friend was truly searching for an answer, replied. "I'm willing to tell you about the Treasure that fills my life, if you really want to know."

Harvest sneered. "This should be good. We are not catching anything anyway, so listening to your story has got to be more entertaining than watching my bait disappear from my hook. Okay, tell me: What is the Treasure that occupies your life?"

Vessel had known Harvest for years, but only recently had they become the best of friends. Although Vessel often shared the love of God with Harvest, Vessel had used wisdom in revealing all of the Treasure within him, understanding not everyone who graciously receives God's love is willing to be watered with the Treasure of who He Is. Vessel hesitated a few moments and then said, "It's like this. I … I am a treasure chest."

Harvest smiled and rolled his eyes. Taking joy in the razzing, he said to his friend, "Oh, so now you're a treasure chest? Well, that explains everything. If you're a treasure chest, it only stands to reason you would be filled with treasure!"

Enjoying his friend's sense of humor, Vessel returned the smile and continued. "Have you heard the Bible story about the time Jesus sat and talked with the woman at the well?"

"Sure. When I was little my neighbors took me to Vacation Bible School every summer. I learned a lot about the stories in the Bible, but I don't recall all of the details," Harvest answered.

"That's fine," Vessel assured. "I'll refresh your memory, and we'll use that story to reveal the Treasure that fills my life."

Altar

Faith

VESSEL has many scriptures committed to memory, yet for this conversation he reached down and retrieved his Bible from his gear. This surprised Harvest a bit, as he had been unaware Vessel carried a Bible in his fishing bag. But Harvest said nothing, as he always respected others and those with faith in God.

As Vessel searched for a particular page, he began explaining to Harvest that in Jesus' day, for a man of Jewish heritage to socialize with the people of Samaria was to break with tradition, especially if he socialized with a woman in public.

However Jesus set aside all tradition and sat down beside a woman of Samaria, at a well of water and said to her, "Give Me a drink."

"The woman was familiar with tradition, so she questioned why Jesus was asking her for a drink. This is how Jesus replied to the woman," Vessel said. Then he read aloud:

> Jesus answered and said to her, "If you knew the
> gift of God, and who it is who says to you, 'Give

Me a drink,' you would have asked Him and He would have given you living water."

—John 4:10

The woman knew Jesus did not have anything with which to draw water from the well, so she asked Him where He would get the living water. Vessel continued:

> Jesus answered and said to her, "Whoever drinks of this water will thirst again, but whoever drinks of the water that I shall give him will never thirst. But the water that I shall give him will become in him a fountain of water springing up into everlasting life."
>
> The woman said to Him, "Sir, give me this water, that I may not thirst, nor come here to draw."
>
> —John 4:13–15

Looking up from his Bible, Vessel said, "This is where the story takes a twist. Jesus was the One who suggested she ask Him for a drink, yet when the woman asked Jesus for the living water, He did not respond to her request right away."

"Instead, Jesus changed the subject of the conversation and revealed to the women that He knew her; He knew her past and her present. Although He knew all things, good and bad, He was in complete fellowship with her, accepting her just as she was with His love, without judgment or condemnation. And He, the Son of the living God, was offering her living water."

"After Jesus made it perfectly clear to the woman that He knew her past and her present situation, He spoke further with her giving her His wisdom and knowledge of Father God."

"Can you imagine, Harvest, the Son of the living God sitting down beside you and having an in-depth conversation with you? Actually sitting and talking to you, just as you are, about the desires of the heavenly Father?"

"I doubt He would pick me," Harvest replied.

"Oh, Harvest, that is not true. Nor was it true for the woman at the well. She probably would not have thought He would pick her either. But that is exactly what Jesus did. She was a person whom others might have called unworthy, yet God loved her so much that He sent His Son to offer her living water."

"As the woman heard the truth in Jesus' words that day, her faith began to increase, drawing her to Jesus like a deer drawn to water," Vessel said. Then he read:

> The woman said to Him, "I know that Messiah is coming (who is called Christ). When He comes, He will tell us all things."
> —John 4:25

There it was, the answer to her request. Jesus led the woman directly to what she had asked Him for. His loving words led her straight to the living water.

Then,

> Jesus said to her, "I who speak to you am He."
>   —John 4:26

The voice of Jesus' testimony declaring who He Is, is the living water." Vessel expounded. "You see Harvest, when Jesus testified 'I who speak to you am He,' declaring to the woman, 'I am the Christ'; the voice of His testimony, was the life giving water she had asked from Him. Jesus is Life. Therefore, whoever drinks the voice of His testimony 'will never thirst and will have eternal life'."

At that moment, Vessel's fishing line tugged. He quickly put his Bible aside and began reeling in what he hoped was a big red. However, he was slightly disappointed to find yet another baby trout. Both men sighed and rolled their eyes at the catch as Vessel worked to return the fish safely back into the water.

After Vessel had recast his line, Harvest inquired, "So the woman was to drink the testimony of Jesus like water?"

"Yes. It may sound unusual, but we drink the testimony of others every day. We heard and believed the weatherman's report today; that is, we actually took in and drank his testimony that it would be a beautiful day. We believed his words."

Harvest grumbled, "Yes, the weatherman's report turned out to be correct. It's the fisherman's report of redfish running which remains in question."

"Yes, I agree." Vessel chuckled. "Fortunately, the words of Jesus' testimony, the Son of the living God, are so true, they are living, giving life to all people who drink of them by believing His testimony." Then, with confidence, Vessel declared, "I have drank living water. I believe in the testimony of Jesus Christ."

"I believe God is real," Harvest said with skepticism. "I'm just not sure I have the faith to fully believe the way you believe."

"Not to worry," assured Vessel. "God is faithful! "Therefore when we hear God's word, the Treasure of faith He Is, comes to us and fills our lives with all the faith we need to truly believe in Him."

Harvest took in every word spoken by his friend, but he did not yet know how to respond. Contemplating his thoughts he sheepishly nodded. "So … it is the Treasure of faith that fills your space."

Vessel smiled. "Yes, it does. But that's not all. There is much more to the Treasure that lives within me."

Laver

Peace

AFTER a relatively quiet lunch, the men recommenced fishing. As they baited their hooks, Harvest inquired, "Isn't that enough?"

"Yes, I am stuffed. That sandwich was huge!" Vessel replied.

Harvest shook his head. "Not the sandwich. Isn't having faith in Jesus enough? I've always heard people say, 'All you need is to believe in Jesus.' How could there be more to the Treasure inside you?"

Vessel quickly responded. "To have believing faith in Jesus Christ is all a person needs to never thirst again. Even so, there is so much more to the Treasure living within me."

Harvest was focused on his fishing line, but he gave Vessel a quick, curious glance.

To clarify his meaning, Vessel asked, "Do you recall when Jesus was on the cross? They hung Him between two other men, criminals who being crucified for their crimes."

Harvest respectfully nodded. "Yes, I've seen several movies regarding the passion of Christ."

Vessel continued. "Then I am sure you recall those two men hanging beside Jesus on the cross were close enough to communicate with Him. They witnessed all of the people mocking Jesus because of His testimony.

Taking up his Bible again, Vessel read:

> Then one of the criminals who were hanged blasphemed Him, saying, "If You are the Christ save Yourself and us."
>
> But the other, answering, rebuked him, saying, "Do you not even fear God, seeing you are under the same condemnation? And we indeed justly, for we receive the due reward of our deeds; but this Man has done nothing wrong."
>
> Then he said to Jesus, "Lord, remember me when You come into Your kingdom." And Jesus said to him, "Assuredly, I say to you, today you will be with Me in Paradise."
>
> —Luke 23:39–43

Harvest, both of the men heard the testimony of Jesus. Both men were given the opportunity to believe. Yet only one of the men used the Treasure of faith given to Him by God to believe."

Vessel recast his fishing line and continued. "Jesus told the woman at the well, 'When a person drinks of the living water, it will become a fountain springing up into everlasting life'. This is what happened to the one man on the cross. As the man drank the living water, believing the testimony of Jesus, the living water became a fountain springing up out of him. Life sprang out of his voice as he confessed, testifying Jesus as Lord, saying 'Lord, remember me when You come into Your kingdom.'"

"The words Jesus spoke to the woman at the well, saying to her those who drink of the living water will receive everlasting life, were confirmed as Jesus said to the man on the cross, "Assuredly, I say to you, today you will be with Me in Paradise."

Harvest, deep in thought about the things his friend was teaching him, asked, "So, even though the man was guilty by his own admission and deserved punishment by death, Jesus simply accepted his confession of faith?"

"Yes," Vessel answered "Without question or condemnation. When the man on the cross believed and confessed Jesus as Lord, he received everlasting life, which Jesus promised with His words, 'today you will be with Me in Paradise'. This was not because of what the man had done, but because he believed the testimony of Jesus with his heart, confessing on the cross Jesus as Lord.

> For with the heart one believes unto righteousness, and with the mouth confession is made unto salvation.
>
> —Rom. 10:10

Harvest began flipping through the live well in search of the perfect bait. After a while, he uttered, "I have question for you, but if you laugh, you're swimming home."

Vessel grinned. "Ask your question and I'll do my best not to swim home."

"I'm almost embarrassed to ask," Harvest admitted. "I don't know if you know, but Christians sometimes speak using words others don't fully understand, presuming everyone around them knows what they're talking about. Those of us who are uncertain of the meanings don't dare ask for fear of being condemned, or worse, preached to. So we simply don't ask."

Before responding, Vessel leaned back, gazed into the water and analyzed the truth of his friend's words. He was aware all too often, he communicated based on his own understanding of God, not the understanding of others—or worse, he didn't communicate the message of Jesus to others at all. With humility, Vessel acknowledged, "There is truth in your observation. I assure you, this is not the impression our heavenly Father would like His children to create. Please forgive me for any inconsiderateness or exclusion on my part. It was never my intent to exclude anyone. Please feel free to ask me any question you may have."

Harvest appreciated his friend's honesty. He hesitated for a moment, but finally spoke. "'Born again.' What is it to be 'born again'? I mean, I know the meaning, but … what is it, really?"

"A man once asked me if I was born again. I answered yes, but truthfully, I didn't know what to say. I felt like he wanted me to say yes, so I did. After all, I know who Jesus is and I know several Bible stories. So I thought, Sure, maybe I am born again."

Thoughts raced through Vessel's mind. He was pleased his friend would ask him such an important question, yet he was insecure about his ability to properly communicate the message of being born again. Then he remembered Jesus, the One who had graciously and simply communicated the message. Turning once again to his Bible, Vessel said, "Harvest, you have asked a good question. A man named Nicodemus who was a leader of the Jewish people asked Jesus a similar question. I'll read His answer to you."

> Jesus answered, "Most assuredly, I say to you, unless one is born of water and the Spirit, he cannot enter the kingdom of God."
> —John 3:5

We are born anew of the Spirit as we believe with our heart the testimony of Jesus, that He Is the Son of the Living God, and we are born of water as our voice testifies the confession of who He Is."

> Therefore, if anyone is in Christ, he is a new creation; old things have passed away; behold, all things have become new.
> —2 Cor. 5:17

Harvest gasped. "Your line—you've got a bite!"

Vessel set his Bible aside and grabbed his pole. "Wahoo! I've got a bite! Get the net. This is a big one."

Vessel was right. It was a big redfish. Both of the men were overwhelmed with joy. It was large enough to be dinner, so they safely stored it away, then quickly recast their lines. They had caught one big red. Certainly there were more out there just waiting to be caught.

As time passed, both men remained mostly silent as they reeled in not one, but two more well-sized redfish. They sent the smallest one back out to sea for another day.

Harvest used the time to reflect on what he had learned. After a while, he inquired, "Who do you make your confession to?"

Gathering his thoughts, Vessel echoed, "Who do you make your confession to? Well, salvation is an intimate relationship between you and the Lord. It is He alone who is worthy to hear the testimony of our confession. However, one hopes all who believe are given the opportunity to share with others the testimony of who He Is. Yet, if a person is not given the opportunity, like the man on the cross beside Jesus, then certainly confessing only to the Lord is enough."

"One thing is certain: when people drink of the living water, truly believing in the testimony of Jesus Christ as Lord, the living water will become a fountain in them, joyfully springing up the testimony of who He Is, for the entire world to hear."

Then Vessel looked at his watch. "It's getting late. Let's head home."

Before he could say anything more, Harvest blurted out, "'Saved'—what is it to be saved?" Christians say, 'They are saved from the curse of the law.' I'm not sure I know all the laws. Do people need to learn the laws first, before they can be saved?"

Vessel laughed gently. Harvest quickly reminded Vessel of the warning he would swim home if he laughed at Harvest's questions. Certain he did not want to swim home, Vessel swiftly said, "I didn't laugh. I smiled really big. I couldn't help it. Your questions have been a cheerful reminder of the 'good' in the good news."

Pulling up anchor, Vessel continued. "What is it to be saved? Jesus explained it best." Knowing these Scriptures by heart Vessel quoted:

> For God so loved the world that He gave His only begotten Son, that whoever believes in Him should not perish but have everlasting life. For God did not send His Son into the world to condemn the world, but that the world through Him might be saved.
>
> —John 3:16–17

The message of Jesus is forever consistent and without contradiction. Whoever believes, confessing Jesus is Lord is saved - saved from perishing - and given everlasting life."

"The apostle Paul also taught the consistent message of Jesus as he explained salvation in this way:

> That if you confess with your mouth the Lord Jesus and believe in your heart that God has raised Him from the dead, you will be saved. For with the heart one believes unto righteousness, and with the mouth confession is made unto salvation.
> —Rom. 10:9–10

Believe in who He Is, confess the Lord Jesus with your mouth, and you will be born again. You will be saved."

Harvest quietly muttered, "People say you have to change your ways if you want to be saved. Doesn't a person need to change their way of living before they can be saved?"

"People do say that, but it is not His truth. No one can change his ways without knowing the Way, nor can a person be saved based upon the way they live; it is with the heart that one believes unto righteousness. We have the peace of right standing with God, because Jesus gave us the Treasure of peace He Is." The Scriptures say:

> Therefore, having been justified by faith, we have peace with God through our Lord Jesus Christ.
> —Rom. 5:1

By this time the men had reached the dock and were out of the boat, tugging and pulling it forward to secure it. Short of breath, Vessel grunted. "You ask about the law. Did you need to learn the law prior to being saved? God is the One who secures us and protects us by teaching us His law. Just as the Treasure of hope, faith, and peace are gifts given to us through Him, so has His law been given to us through Him. His promise to us is:

> …..I will put My laws in their mind and write them on their hearts; and I will be their God, and they shall be My people.
>
> —Heb. 8:10

Certainly, the Lord uses His Holy word to teach us, as well as the voice of His people to testify of who He Is just as I have testified of Him to you today. Yet it is God alone who inscribes our hearts and minds with His laws."

It had been a long hot day, so the drive home was very quiet: mostly chitchat about the new tires Harvest had recently bought for his truck and how he needed to get the air-conditioning repaired before summer.

When Vessel got out of the truck and said good-bye, Harvest replied, "I've learned a lot today. Thanks. It gives a man something to think about."

Candlestick

Joy

EARLY the next Saturday, Vessel anxiously waited with fishing gear in hand for Harvest to pick him up. It was much cooler than normal so he was glad when he saw his friend soaring up the drive.

As Vessel walked briskly toward the truck, Harvest did something he had never done before. He got out gave Vessel a big smile, and said, "Good morning! Are you ready to catch the big one?" Vessel was a little uncertain. He nodded and continued toward the truck.

Harvest had been picking Vessel up every Saturday for the past several weeks, yet not once had he gotten out of the truck with an early morning greeting. Not being a morning person, Harvest normally did not say much until they had unloaded and were trolling down river. But today—today was different.

Vessel loaded his gear into the back of the truck, and Harvest talked. He said although the cold front had moved in, the winds were calm and the river was smooth as glass.

Vessel raised his eyebrows. He knew something was up with Harvest, although he wasn't sure what.

Before Vessel even got his seatbelt on, Harvest said, "I did it!" He was beaming.

"Did what?" asked Vessel.

"I told God I believe. I believe He sent His Jesus to die for me. I believe the testimony of Jesus. I believe He Is my Savior! And you know what? I don't care what anyone else believes or thinks! This is what I believe." Without taking a breath, Harvest continued. "I spent a lot of time thinking about the things you and I discussed last week. I studied the Scriptures you shared with me, especially the ones in the book of John about how God loved me so much that He gave His only begotten Son not to condemn me, but to die for me."

"John 3:16–17," confirmed Vessel.

"Yes. I thought I might have believed in Jesus when I was a child, yet I was unsure I could ever truly believe. But with His faith, I believe!"

"And I confessed to God 'I believe.' So that's it! I am saved! I am born again!"

Overwhelmed with joy, Vessel responded, "Harvest, that's great! I'm happy for you. It is so good to see your light shining."

Harvest was a little taken aback. "What light?"

"Jesus! He Is the light of the world, and because you received Him as Lord of your life, He now lives in you and His light is shining through you. Remember we talked about how I am filled with the Treasure? Now that you have confessed Jesus as Lord, you too are filled with the Treasure. And believe me, the Treasure of joy He Is, is shining through you this morning."

Harvest looked at himself in the rearview mirror. "You can see it?"

Vessel laughed. "I don't know about in your rearview mirror, but the Scripture says, "As in water face reflects face, so a man's heart reveals the man" (Prov. 27:19). Undoubtedly, your heart is a nice reflection of Him in you this morning. And the voice of your testimony, springing up out of you, declaring who He Is, is your heart's way of revealing the joy of Christ in you. It is as the prophet Isaiah said:

> I will greatly rejoice in the Lord, my soul shall be joyful in my God; for He has clothed me with the garments of salvation, He has covered me with the robe of righteousness.
>
> —Isa. 61:10

Table of Showbread

Righteousness

TROLLING around the islands, Harvest inquired, "Now that I know, He Is my Lord, I want to do all the good He wants me to do. So, what should I do?"

"Don't sweat it!" Vessel answered.

"Don't sweat it?" echoed Harvest.

"That's right. Don't sweat it. That is the perfect will of God."

"God sent His Son Jesus to sweat for us. We are simply to receive all the goodness He labored to provide," Vessel stated.

Harvest patiently baited his hook and asked, "How do we do that?"

"By letting go of our efforts and labors of good, and receiving the good He has already labored to give us. You see, Harvest, in the beginning God labored, creating all the good of heaven and the earth, including a bountiful garden of trees which overflowed with good fruit."

"God gave Adam and Eve access to freely eat of all the trees in His garden, yet by His divine and loving protection He commanded them not to eat from the tree of the knowledge of good and evil. God is Divine and He knew if Adam and Eve ate from the tree, they would be like God, and they would have the knowledge of good and evil. It was never God's will for His beautiful creation to know good and evil. Unfortunately Adam and Eve ate from the tree and now all mankind has the knowledge of good and evil."

"I understand why God would not want us to know evil, but why wouldn't God want us to know good?" Harvest questioned.

"The trouble with knowing good is that mankind is not capable of accomplishing the expectation of good. Therefore our conscience constantly reminds us that we are not good enough. It is because we know 'good' and 'evil' that we also know the cruelty of guilt and condemnation."

Harvest listening intently, keeping an eye on his fishing line said, "Go on."

"God's perfect will was and always has been that His children not labor to earn right standing with Him nor eat from the tree of knowledge of good and evil. This is why God prepared for us the body of His Son, Jesus." Taking up his Bible, Vessel explained, "Adam and Eve surrendered to their own selfish will in the Garden of Eden. Jesus surrendered to the will of God in the garden of Gethsemane and prayed saying:

...O My Father, if it is possible let this cup pass
from Me; nevertheless, not as I will but as You will.
—Matt. 26:39

It was the will of the Father, for Jesus to drink the sin our
unbelief which caused Jesus great agony;

And being in agony, He prayed more earnestly.
Then His sweat became like great drops of blood
falling down to the ground.
—Luke 22:44

The first drops of blood the body of Jesus shed came from
own His sweat in the garden of Gethsemane. And as the
water of His sweat turned to blood, it became the testimony
that Jesus is the One who labored for us. Our effort of
sweat and good deeds can never earn what Jesus has already
labored for us, in His flesh:

Surely He has borne our griefs and carried our
sorrows; yet we esteemed Him stricken, smitten by
God, and afflicted. But He was wounded for our
transgressions, He was bruised for our iniquities;
the chastisement for our peace was upon Him,
and by His stripes we are healed.
—Isa. 53:4–5

Jesus gave us the Treasure of righteousness He Is; we are in
right standing with God not because of our labor, but His.
He Is the Lord our Righteousness."

The wind was picking up, so Harvest leaned back and rested secure on the boat. With a mischievous grin, he said, "Well, I've always wanted to forget my labor, sit back, relax, and fish all day."

Vessel laughed at his friend. "No, no, I didn't say to do nothing. I said all the good God requires of us has been accomplished by Jesus and His bountiful provision is provided for us daily by our heavenly Father."

"However, the good we are called to do for the love of mankind is great and the opportunities to do good for others is endless. But again, rest assured, all the good required of us by God has already been accomplished by Jesus."

Just then, a gust of wind swirled around, rocking the boat, so Vessel recommended, "Let's go ashore and fish from the island."

Altar of Incense

Blessing

SEAGULLS flurried as the men set up their fishing poles on the shore and chatted about how fishing from the island would give them the space needed to reel in a really big catch.

Their prediction turned out to be right. After only an hour they had caught several fish—not redfish, but a few well-sized trout, all of which they released safely back into the water since their families would be having dinner tonight at the local Christmas festival.

Yet it was still early morning, so, with high hopes of catching a big red, Vessel recast his line.

Harvest decided to take a walk along the island to check out the flamingos hidden in the cove and to give him time to reflect on the conversation he and Vessel had earlier regarding the bountiful provision of Jesus, our righteousness.

When Harvest returned, Vessel had not moved from his favorite fishing spot.

Harvest took a seat on the coral rock beside him and asked, "How do you pray? I mean, I know how to pray, but how do *you* pray?"

"I simply talk to the Lord, just as I am talking to you," Vessel replied. He tugged his fishing line and proceeded. "With that said, I do respect our Lord as Holy, therefore when I pray I humble myself before Him and pray the prayer Jesus taught us to pray. He said:

> In this manner, therefore pray:
>
> Our Father in heaven, Hallowed be Your name.
> Your kingdom come, Your will be done on earth as it is in heaven.
> Give us this day our daily bread.
> And forgive us our debts as we forgive our debtors.
> And do not lead us into temptation, but deliver us from the evil one.
> For Yours is the kingdom and the power and the glory forever. Amen.
>
> —Matt. 6:9–13

After taking a deep breath Vessel added, "Harvest, I believe if we pray in Jesus name, the prayer Jesus taught us to pray, that it could be the only prayer we would ever need to pray. When His prayer is spoken through us, the Treasure of blessing He Is, is glorified through the voice of our prayer."

"Just as it was with Moses and the children of Israel, after they had been set free from slavery and crossed through the waters of the Red Sea," Vessel expounded. "The children of Israel walked in complete liberty, rejoicing and praising the Lord for three days. On the third day they found water, but the children of God could not drink because the water was bitter."

"What did they do?" inquired Harvest.

"They did what most of us do. They complained!" Vessel answered with a smile. "Fortunately for them, though, Moses had spent enough time with God that He knew what they were supposed to do."

"What's that?" Harvest asked with anticipation.

"Moses cried out to the Lord for help!" Then, not knowing the Scripture by heart, Vessel reached down to get his Bible and read Moses's cry.

> So he cried out the Lord, and the Lord showed Him a tree. When he (Moses) cast it (the tree) into the waters, the waters were made sweet…
>
> —Ex.15:25

When Moses cried out, the Lord showed Moses the witness of His blessing that was already there, waiting for His children before they ever met their need. The Lord was simply waiting with anticipation to hear the call of His children, that He might reveal the glory of the Treasure of blessing He Is."

Vessel continued, "The tree the Lord showed Moses was an actual tree, yet for us it is a typology or sign signifying the sweet redemption of Jesus Christ. That is why the tree Moses used not only took away the bitterness in the water, but also made the water sweet. When Moses placed the tree in the bitter water, it was made sweet, testifying of how the sweet redemption of Jesus healed the testimony of guilt and condemnation which once stood before us with His own body, and blessed us with the sweet healing of His righteousness." The Scripture says:

> Who Himself bore our sins in His own body on the tree, that we, having died to sins, might live for righteousness – by whose stripes you were healed.
>
> —1 Pet. 2:24

Veil

Grace

THE warmth of the sun beamed down on the men as they proceeded to fish. When out of nowhere, a speedboat buzzed by, sending a mass of cold waves over the little island and completely soaked their feet and all of their belongings.

Harvest was so mad he yelled at the speed boat and the waves. "What is wrong with people?" He swore. "How could anyone be so inconsiderate?" shouted Harvest as he quickly helped Vessel gather all of their belongings before they washed into the deep, continuing to swear with displeasure.

It was only after the men had dried everything off and begun to warm their feet in the sun that Harvest looked at Vessel and muttered, "Sorry, but they made me angry."

"No worries. It made me angry, too."

"Yeah, but you kept your cool."

"I didn't get the chance to lose my cool. By the time you simmered down and stopped steaming, there was nothing hot left for me to vent." They both broke out into laughter.

Harvest checked his fishing line only to find the waves had taken his good bait. He huffed, sighed then humbly he asked, "So, when we do things we know are not pleasing to our Father, such as … maybe my reaction to the speedboat … how do we go about making something like that right with Him?"

"It might surprise you, but I believe our Lord understands appropriate anger," Vessel replied. "I'm not saying swearing at the waves and the speedboat were necessarily appropriate anger, but nonetheless, I believe He is sympathetic to the situations we face in this world."

"Nevertheless, when I do something that might be displeasing to Him, I go straight to Him. Without condemnation or hesitation, I just go straight to my heavenly Father and talk to Him about it."

"What do you say to Him?" inquired Harvest.

With a mischievous chuckle, Vessel replied, "Well, honestly, sometimes—often times—I start out by giving Him all of my excuses as to why I did what I did. And then, after spending time in His presence, I humble myself in prayer to Him who is gracious to forgive."

Deep in thought, Harvest sat back down on the coral rock and asked, "What if we do something really bad? Something we know our heavenly Father would not be pleased with?"

"No matter what we do, no matter how big or small it is, we are to come boldly before His throne of grace without fear," Vessel assured. "It is His grace that restores and heals the harm we have brought upon ourselves and to others."

Relaxed and enjoying the rays of the sun, Harvest dug his toes into the sand and echoed, "Boldly before His throne of grace?"

"Yes," confirmed Vessel. "The honor of boldly entering into the throne of His of grace has been given to us at great cost. Jesus gave His life so that no matter what sin we commit, we are free to boldly enter into the presence of His grace without fear, guilt, or condemnation."

"Prior to Jesus dying for us on the cross, only the High Priest was granted access to enter the Holy place of the presence of God. But because Jesus gave His life for us, we have now been given access to enter into His grace. The Scripture declares:

> Let us therefore come boldly to the throne of
> grace, that we may obtain mercy and find grace
> to help in time of need.
>
> —Heb. 4:16

Jesus death removed all that separated us from the holiest place of God, allowing us access to enter His presence of grace. The Scripture gives us many signs that testify to how Jesus removed all that separated us from His Holy presence. I consider the most revealing sign to be when Jesus gave up His spirit and died upon the cross. The Scripture says:

> But one of the soldiers pierced His side with a
> spear, and immediately blood and water came out.
> —John 19:34

When the soldier pierced the flesh of Jesus, blood and water came out of His body. The blood separated from the water. That was physical evidence to all those who witnessed it that Jesus had truly died upon the cross; it was a visual sign testifying of His grace."

"I got one, I got a big one!" Harvest suddenly yelped.

Vessel jumped up eagerly. "Bring him in, bring him in, don't lose him, he's a big one!"

Sure enough, the fish Harvest reeled in turned out to be the biggest fish they had caught in months. It was not a red, but a really big snook.

"Man, is he a big one!" Vessel bragged, snapping a picture of Harvest's great catch. Harvest grinned from ear to ear as he returned his best catch safely back in the water.

There was a long silence as the men basked in the excitement of catching such a big fish. Then Harvest said, "Before I caught the most awesome fish of the day, you were telling me how Jesus death on the cross gave us access to the presence of His grace. My quandary is I don't fully understand grace."

Vessel smiled and replied, "Well, Harvest, to be honest with you, His grace is so incredibly immeasurable that I am not certain any of God's children can fully understand the magnitude of His amazing grace. However, I can tell you a Bible story about the time the apostle Peter found His grace."

"Okay," said Harvest, as he leaned back to rest in the sun.

"Peter was one of the people closest to Jesus during Jesus ministry on earth. Yet, when Jesus was arrested, Peter, in an attempt to save himself, completely denied knowing Jesus. Not just once, but three times! When the accusers asked Peter if he knew Jesus, Peter lied, cursed, and denied knowing His friend, utterly betraying Jesus. Nevertheless, when Jesus was resurrected from the grave, He returned and visited His disciples, including Peter."

"On one of His visits, the disciples had been out at sea, fishing all night. When they returned, Jesus was standing on the shoreline waiting to meet them. From the shore, He called out, 'Have you caught any fish?' They responded no, so Jesus called out to them again, saying, 'Cast the net on the right side of the boat, and you will find some.' When the disciples followed Jesus instruction, they caught so many fish that they were not able to draw the net back into the boat."

"That was a big catch," Harvest interjected.

"Yes, the Bible calls it 'a multitude of fish,' Vessel explained and continued. "When Peter realized the man on the shore waiting for them was Jesus, Peter plunged into the water and swam directly to Jesus, leaving behind the other disciples and the big catch Jesus had just given to them."

"Peter knew it could only be by His grace that Jesus was waiting to meet with him. All of the disciples found grace in the presence of Jesus that day, yet it was Peter who recognized the privilege of plunging into the water and boldly rushing to be in the presence of His grace."

Vessel paused, taking the time to appreciate the significance of the story. "I believe Jesus standing on the shoreline, waiting for Peter and the disciples, is one of the most beautiful illustrations of His heart of grace. And just as Jesus waited for them that morning, so does He wait for us to plunge into the testimony of who He Is and find His grace."

Harvest remained relaxed in the sun with eyes closed. "Wouldn't it be more accurate to say Grace found them? After all, Jesus was there before they were, waiting for them."

"True," agreed Vessel. "Grace did find them. Jesus was there before they arrived, waiting for them. Just as the Lord had already supplied the tree to make the bitter water sweet for His children. And just as our Father awaits our prayer to glorify the Treasure of blessing He Is, so does our Lord wait for us to come to Him that He might lavish us with the eternal Treasure of grace He Is."

Mercy Seat

Mercy

Hours later, Harvest and Vessel were loading the boat in preparation to leave, when out of nowhere, the speedboat which had buzzed them earlier came around the corner of the island at a very slow speed.

One of the men on the speed boat sheepishly called out, "Hey, do you have anything extra to drink? We traveled further than expected and are a quite a distance from our dock. We'll pay you."

Vessel called back, "Sure, we have extra water. You're welcome to it, free of charge!" Vessel smiled and waded out through the cold to hand the men the bottled water.

Harvest, on the other hand, did not even look up. He could not believe the audacity of the men even asking. After what they had done earlier, buzzing the island, how could they even ask?

The men on the boat took the water, thanked Vessel, and slowly drove away.

As Vessel waded back, Harvest called out, "I know our heavenly Father would have wanted us to give them the water, but really, couldn't you at least have made them get out of the boat and walk to you through the cold water?"

Vessel smiled. "Harvest, I know they did not deserve our mercy, and I know if they had not needed us, they probably would have laughed and buzzed right by us again. Nevertheless, our heavenly Father expects us to be merciful to others, as He Is merciful to us. The scripture says, 'Blessed are the merciful, for they shall obtain mercy' (Matt. 5:7)."

Just then, a baby manatee swam by, gently rubbing up against Vessel. He was startled by the gesture of the newborn calf and overwhelmed by the joy of its presence.

Harvest was also excited to see the magnificent mammal with its mother calf just behind it. He waded into the water for a closer look, also handing Vessel a towel for warmth. "Next time, I want to be the one who shows mercy."

Vessel smiled, wrapped himself in the towel, and sat upon the coral rock, as Harvest began loading their gear in the boat. Vessel said "Whenever I am hesitant about being merciful to others, I always think of Jesus who, when He knew all things had been accomplished on the cross, said, 'I thirst.'"

"It was at that time, Harvest, that Jesus gave tremendous testimony of His mercy. Jesus, who was in sheer agony, dying on the cross, testified for all to hear of His mercy." Vessel cleared his throat and pushed back tears. "The One who proclaimed to the woman at the well 'whoever drinks of the water that I shall give him will never thirst' and to His followers 'he who believes in Me shall never thirst' Himself testified on the cross, 'I thirst'."

"Harvest, those two words spoken by the Son of God is surely the greatest words ever spoken of His mercy. His testimony of His thirst was and is His merciful declaration that He took the thirst of the entire world. Because of Jesus, all who believe in Him will never thirst; we will always have within us the testimony of who He Is."

"Moreover for those who have not yet taken a drink of the words of His testimony, He patiently waits. He waits on them to believe in Him so that He might lavish them with all of His mercy."

As they loaded their remaining items onto the boat, Harvest declared, "I sure am glad His mercy waited on me."

"I'm glad He waited on me too," agreed Vessel. "And it is with joy that we know He continues to wait for us to find His grace and obtain His mercy."

"If His mercy is waiting on me, I want to take it. How do I do that?" Harvest asked eagerly.

Taking their seats on the boat, Vessel looked out over the water, took a deep breath, and said, "Harvest, you ask the best questions. Fortunately for all of us, Jesus taught us by His words and by His actions. By His words, 'I thirst,' we know He Is our provision of mercy. And by His actions, we know how to obtain His mercy."

"You see, the disciples not only found His grace on the shore fishing that morning, they also obtained His mercy."

"When the disciples arrived on shore, Jesus said to them, 'Come and eat breakfast'. He who had suffered excruciating pain at the cross for all of them, all of us, was serving them breakfast! He was not asking of them, yet with absolute mercy, He was giving to them. All the disciples had to do to obtain His mercy was to reach out and take it from His nail scared hands."

Harvest interjected, "Wow, taking breakfast from His nail scared hands must have been a humbling experience for the disciples."

As the men pushed off the island, Vessel replied, "The Treasure of mercy He Is, is so incredibly undeserved the only way to obtain it, is to humbly reach into His nail-scarred hands and take it."

"As the Son of man, grace gave all. As the Son of God, mercy denied nothing."

Ark

Rest

THE next Friday, Vessel and Harvest were both excited, as it was just days before Christmas and they were both off work for the Holiday. Today they would be spending the day deep-sea fishing with Captain Surv. Surv had been a friend of Vessel's for years. He was a burly sea captain, professional fisherman, and Bible teacher at Vessel's church. Harvest had just met Surv last week at Sunday school.

The purpose of the fishing trip was to have a fun yet productive day because their families were counting on them to bring home enough fish to feed all of them at a big Christmas cookout. And that was going to require a really big catch. They couldn't have asked for a better forecast; the weatherman called for a high of seventy-two degrees and calm winds. They just knew it would be a great day for fishing.

Their prediction was correct. By noon, the men had already caught several big fish: three large red snappers and one really large yellow fin tuna. The tuna was the best catch of the day. Surv had brought it in, but all three were beaming with the pride of such a fine-looking catch.

As grateful as they were for the good fishing, they were also exhausted by it. Out of sheer exhaustion, the men decided to rest a short time in the sun before heading home. All three lay back in their deck chairs, little expecting they would all fall asleep.

Less than an hour later, they awoke to discover the sky had turned grey and the wind had picked up. Concerned by the quick change in the weather, they contacted base and found their fears were true: a tropical storm was quickly developing over the coast. The forecast predicted the storm would pass well before sunset and would be stronger on shore than off, only skirting their current location at sea.

Surv's boat was a luxury deep sea fishing boat with enough room for the three of them to rest comfortable through the storm so the men determined it was best to batten down the hatches and ride out the storm at sea.

Below deck Vessel and Surv chose to snack and play a game of chess, Harvest on the other hand decided it was best to anxiously pace the floor.

After a few minutes Surv said, "Harvest you might as well sit down and rest there is nothing more we can do." "Rest!" Harvest exclaimed. "Resting is why we are in this situation. How could we have all three fallen asleep?"

"Because all three of us were tired," answered Vessel.

Harvest sighed "It was a senseless waste of time, we could have rested tonight."

Surv swirled his hot cocoa and said "Harvest, did you know God rested? He worked six days creating heaven and earth and then on the seventh day He rested."

Harvest acknowledged "I guess I never thought about it."

Surv continued. "God is the creator and giver of rest, therefore when we receive the Treasure of rest, He Is, we give honor to Him as being the One who rests in His accomplishment of all things good."

Vessel chimed in, "If Jesus was here He would sleep right through this storm. Jesus understood the value of rest."

"Yes, He did" Surv replied "There was a time Jesus and the disciples were out at sea and a windstorm came upon them so strong waves of water came onto the boat. The disciples feared for their lives, but Jesus slept. The disciples feared so much they woke Jesus and asked Him 'do you not care that we perish!' Jesus asked them 'why are you fearful, O you of little faith?' Then Jesus rebuked the winds and the sea saying 'Peace, be still' and the wind ceased and there was a great calm."

"Their lives were in jeopardy, shouldn't they have been fearful," asked Harvest?

Surv replied. "It was at Jesus' request that the disciples follow Him to the other side of the sea, therefore Jesus expected His disciples to rest in His direction."

Vessel added, "The winds of negative circumstances may be fierce at times and voices of those whose testimony are contrary to the testimony of who He Is will often rage against us, but we should not fear, yet we should rest in knowing that He who called us to follow Him is well able to see us through to the end."

Harvest, plopped down on the couch fluffed the pillow and said "If I am going to be like Jesus I may as well learn to rest through the storm."

Covenant

Knowledge

AFTER a short while the sun broke through the clouds, so the men came up from the galley. When they arrived back out on deck, shining directly over them was a rainbow with vibrant colors so bright they reflected off of the face of the water. It was a magnificent sight. As they gazed upon the scene, the men each gave the Lord thanks for giving them rest through the storm and for showing them the splendor of His rainbow.

After only a few minutes of enjoying the scene, anxious to get home before sunset, they hurried to inspect the boat for weather damage. Everything was shipshape except for the navigation system, which was shot. Lighting must have hit it.

It took only a second for Harvest to realize the reality of their circumstances. "The storm tossed us all over the sea. How will we get home without the navigation system, which way is home?"

"I have my grandfather's compass. It will lead us home," Surv answered with assurance.

"Oh, great, a state-of-the-art navigation system replaced by an ancient compass," Harvest scoffed.

"Not to worry. The ol' compass will guide us home." Surv said pointing out to sea "What do you see?"

"Not land!" Harvest responded.

Surv walked toward the stern of the boat. Jesting with his new friend, and called out "A magnificent rainbow and an endless amount of water! What a view!"

Vessel chimed in, "It is an impressive view!"

"I get it, I get it. You guys have no concerns about finding our way home, so I'll do my best not to worry either," Harvest stated.

In an effort to take Harvest's mind off of their situation, Vessel pointed to the rainbow. "Did you know God gave Noah the rainbow as a sign of His covenant? The rainbow is the reflection of sunlight in water dropping from the heavens, a visual testimony of God's covenant promise to Noah that never again would all flesh be cut off by the waters of the flood, nor would water flood the earth again."

Surv added, "And just as the Lord made covenant with Noah, He has made a new covenant with us. In His covenant promise to us, He said:

> …..I will put My laws in their mind and write them on their hearts; and I will be their God, and they will be My people. None of them shall teach his neighbor, and none his brother, saying 'Know the LORD,' for all shall know Me, from the

least of them to the greatest of them. For I will be merciful to their unrighteousness, and their sins and their lawless deeds I will remember no more."

—Heb. 8:10–12

He has put the Treasure of knowledge He Is, in our mind and in our heart. He Is the assurance we have deep within us that we know that we know, He Is our God and we are His people."

Vessel interjected. "Today, Surv will use his grandfather's compass to guide us home; yet in life it is the knowledge of Him within us, that guides and protects us through life."

Surv then called out, "Hold on, we're racing the wind home!"

Anointing Oil

Truth

"LOOK, the lighthouse!" shouted Harvest.

At the helm, Surv had already seen the shoreline and was maintaining straight course ahead.

With relief, Harvest put his hands behind his head, leaned back, and said, "I admit it, Surv, I didn't know if your ol' compass could get us home, but now I see the lighthouse." He breathed a deep breath of relief. "Woo! We're almost home. Boy I am relieved!"

Nodding in agreement, Vessel grinned.

A short distance from shore, Surv reduced the speed of the boat. As the noise from the motor reduced, Surv confessed, "We would have seen the lighthouse sooner if I had trusted in the ol' compass a little more than what my eyes could see."

Harvest sat straight up and shrieked. "What?"

Surv apologetically replied, "About an hour ago, I thought I saw the shore. Although the compass did not direct me toward what I was seeing, I steered toward it anyway. As I drew closer, I realized what I was seeing wasn't the shore, but a dark cloud which had settled over the face of the deep."

As not to embarrass himself any further, Surv quickly assured them. "As soon as I realized my eyes had deceived me, I immediately returned my trust solely to the compass."

Vessel realized how much humility it took for an experienced sea captain to admit his mistake, especially since sunset was so very near. Therefore he said, "Well, we've all done that."

"What's that?" inquired Harvest.

"We have all focused on what we could see, other than what we knew as truth only to find a big black cloud of regret, or worse, to find ourselves sinking the way Peter did," answered Vessel.

"Sinking?" Harvest asked.

Vessel explained. "During the time of Jesus ministry on earth, Peter and the disciples were out at sea during yet another storm the winds were so boisterous that the waves began tossing their boat. Jesus was on the shore and saw His disciples in distress, so He stepped out and began walking on the water to be with them. When the disciples looked out and saw Jesus walking on the water, they thought He was a ghost and became even more afraid. Jesus calmed their fears by saying:

….Be of good cheer! It is I, do not be afraid.
—Matt.14:27

As the disciples' watched Jesus walk toward them, Peter called out to Jesus, 'Lord, if it is You, command me to come to You on the water.'"

"Jesus answered Peter's request and called him to 'come.'

At Jesus call, Peter stepped out of the boat and began walking on the water!"

"However as Peter walked upon the water he saw the wind was boisterous, fearful he began to sink, and cried out to Jesus, 'Lord, save me!'"

Surv warmly interjected;

> And immediately Jesus stretched out His hand and caught him, and said to him, 'O you of little faith, why did you doubt?' And when they got into the boat, the wind ceased.
>
> —Matt. 14:31–32

Vessel continued, "Peter may have doubted and begun to sink, but Jesus was already there waiting with out-reached arm, ready to help Peter accomplish the goal in which Jesus had called him to achieve."

"Peter's success did not rest secure upon Peter; it rested secure upon the truth in the word of Jesus call."

"No matter how boisterous the winds in our life blow, or how much we doubt, the word of His call is forever true."

Surv confirmed, "Jesus is Truth. His word is infallible. Whether we are walking by faith upon the truth of His testimony, or fearfully sinking in the doubt of our fears. The Treasure of truth He Is will forever be there waiting to reach out, lift us up and walk with us, that we too will accomplish all His word has called us to do."

Blood

Victory

To avoid holiday traffic, Surv drove the back road home. Normally, the road was very dark. Yet tonight, the men were pleasantly surprised to see almost every home along the way shining bright with the lights of Christmas.

As they drew near Vessel's neighborhood, he stated, "My family will all be asleep when I get home."

"My family will be sleeping too," yawned Harvest. "That is ok though, because checking in on my precious little girls and beautiful wife as they sleep completely overwhelms my heart with gratitude." Harvest expressed, "I am blessed to have such a wonderful family." Then with slight hesitation he added, "Well maybe I should say overwhelmed with gratitude and fear."

"Fear" questioned Surv?

"Yes. Fear that I will fail them," Harvest replied. "Regrettably, I have failed them in the past, to the point I almost lost them. I made some really poor choices a few years ago, and I fear I will return to my past ways, losing my family forever."

"I understand that kind of fear," stated Vessel. "I lived with it for years. That is until my grandmother taught me that God has given us the power to overcome the fear and captivity of our past."

"She taught me that when God saved us, He gave us a new heart. A heart filled with the promise that the blood of Jesus has set us free!"

"Therefore when the fear of our past, challenges our freedom, it is nothing more than our natural heart deceiving us with thoughts of evil."

"And then my grandmother taught me something I have never forgotten. She said, 'When the enemy of your past comes chasing after you, stand firm in liberty, lift up your hands and with the Treasure of victory He Is in your voice, declare the testimony of who He Is in you!'"

Surv, enjoying the conversation suggested, "Vessel, tell Harvest about the time the children of Israel actually saw the salvation of our Lord's overcoming victory."

"It was one of the most magnificent signs God ever showed to reveal the testimony of who He Is." Vessel, sitting straight up stated with confidence, "It was the sign He gave the children of Israel at the Red Sea!"

"The children of Israel had already been set free by the blood of the sacrifice, but the slave master of their past challenged their freedom by continually chasing after them, chasing them all the way to the Red Sea."

"I know that story," replied Harvest. "That's the time the Lord instructed Moses to lift us his rod and stretch out his hand over the sea. And when Moses did as God instructed the waters of the sea parted, creating a safe pathway for the children of God to pass through."

"You're right," Vessel affirmed. "And after the children of Israel safely passed through the water on dry ground, the slave master of their past and his entire army stepped right into the path of God's provision for His children. That was it! The enemy had gone too far!"

"So at the Lord's instruction, Moses stretched out his hand over the sea again and when he did, the water returned with full strength and completely overcame the salve master and his entire army. It was over! Everything that had persistently tried to hold the children of God captive was wiped-out and washed away by the water."

Vessel concluded, "The sign God gave the children of Israel of His victory remains true for us today. The blood of Jesus has set us completely free! And the word of our testimony wipes out anything that tries to hold us captive to our past.

The scripture says;

> And they overcame him by the blood of the Lamb
> and by the word of their testimony, and they did
> not love their lives to the death.
>
> —Rev. 12:11

Cornerstone

Love

THE aroma from Surv's special fish seasonings was flowing all through the park as the children played their games and the adults prepared the Christmas celebration table.

Surv called out, "Gather the children around the table. The fish will be ready soon."

Vessel carried out Surv's request and called the families to the table. To calm the children before the food was served, Vessel asked them if they would like to hear a story about Jesus in celebration of His birthday. Children love stories, so they all cried a rambunctious, "Yes!"

Vessel began His story. "Our heavenly Father loved us so much that He sent His only begotten Son from heaven to be born of the Virgin Mary."

"Mary, the mother of Jesus of course, knew Jesus was the Son of God. Yet, she raised Jesus the same way all the other children of her culture were raised in that time. Jesus lived and played just like all of you. Very few people knew He was the Son of God."

"It wasn't until Jesus was an adult that His glory was revealed. It happened while He was attending a wedding with His mother. The wedding was a celebration a bit like ours today. Friends and family were all gathered together, eating and drinking."

"During the celebration, the mother of Jesus heard that the host had run out of wine for the guests. Knowing her Son was the Son of God; Mary turned to Jesus and asked Him to provide for their need."

"Jesus answered his mom's request—just as He answers for all of us who ask of Him—by providing for them, the very best."

"And He did it by instructing the servants to fill purified vessels with water. And then Jesus instructed the servants to give a drink to the ruler of the feast. When the servants poured the water from the vessel for the ruler of the feast to taste, the water had turned to wine!"

"Jesus had turned water into wine—not just any wine, but the best wine! The ruler of the feast did not know where the wine came from; so he called for the bridegroom and gave him praise for saving the best wine for last."

The children all sat silently, their eyes fixed upon Vessel. They had never heard this Christmas story before.

Surv was listening from the grill. He signaled to Vessel to keep going, the fish could wait.

Vessel continued. "You see, children, it was on that day at the wedding that Jesus first revealed His glory. And He did that by giving the sign which testifies of His love."

"Jesus often taught by telling stories and giving signs so all who heard His teachings would have a visual illustration of who He Is."

"Yet on this day, Jesus taught by a living illustration. You see, when Jesus instructed the servants to fill the empty vessels with water, He was illustrating how by His Spirit, the Father filled an earthen vessel with His Son Jesus in the form of a newborn baby. And when Jesus grew to be an adult He lived His life serving others, filling others to the brim with the living water of His testimony. And at His death, His blood turned the testimony of who He Is into the testimony of His eternal covenant of love."

Vessel's oldest daughter then declared, "The story of Jesus turning water into wine was not just a story in the life of Jesus; it is the story of His life!"

Vessel smiled. "Yes, sweet daughter, it is. And now it is the story we are to tell as we live our life."

"We are to be like Jesus and serve our brothers and sisters in Christ by filling each other to the brim with the testimony of who He Is, just as the servants filled the earthen vessels with water at the wedding."

Surv quietly placed the fish on the table as Vessel continued, "The scripture says we are the body of Christ, vessels which are to be filled with the testimony of who He Is, and we are to allow the testimony of His love to flow from us for the entire world to drink."

Harvest's oldest daughter then asked, "But the entire world does not know Jesus? Shouldn't we first fill them to the brim with the water, the testimony of who He Is, and then just let Jesus turn the testimony into His love?"

Vessel replied, "We can. But look at Jesus' example in this story: although the ruler of the feast did not know Jesus was the Son of God, Jesus instructed the servants to give him the wine."

"When the ruler of the feast tasted the wine, he then called upon the bridegroom to give him praise for saving the best wine for last."

"Scripture reveals to us that in heaven Jesus is the bridegroom. Therefore, when the ruler of the feast gave praise to the bridegroom, it was a sign to us that all those who taste His love will surely bow at the name of Jesus and give Him praise."

Vessel looked at the awesome amount of fish on the table and grinned, "Who wants to say the blessing?"

"I will," Harvest quickly responded. "Father, thank you for loving us and giving to us Your Son Jesus, who fills us with the Treasure of love He Is. We ask You to help us to be more like Jesus, faithfully serving one another by filling each other to the brim with the testimony of who He Is. And as Your vessels of honor, we will freely pour out to the entire world Your love. This Christmas season, we rejoice in the celebration of Your Son, Jesus, Your eternal gift of love. Amen."

"Let's eat!"

Glory

Goodness

AFTER the feast, the laughter of the children playing rose in the air as the adults chatted by the dock of the river, discussing how good Surv's cooking was and how much they all truly enjoyed being together during the Christmas season.

Harvest, however, remained quiet as he gazed over the water. After a while, he muttered, "The Father, the Son, and the Holy Spirit."

At his statement everyone became quiet and turned their eyes toward him. Surv responded, "That is the blessed Trinity of our Lord."

Still pondering his thoughts, Harvest stated, "This is the season we celebrate the birth of our Savior Jesus, the Father's gift of His eternal love."

"Yes," confirmed Vessel.

With a little uncertainty, Harvest inquired. "The Holy Spirit. What about the Holy Spirit? I understand the Father, the Son, and the Holy Spirit are individual, "yet One in unity." But I'm not certain I know Him, you know, *personally*, as an individual."

Surv responded, "As believers, we have all known Holy Spirit from the very beginning of our relationship with our Lord. God the Father is the One who drew us to His Son, Jesus, and Holy Spirit is the One who helped us to see our need for Jesus our Savoir."

"He is the One who testifies of Jesus. And it is because of Him that we now testify, for…no one can say that 'Jesus is Lord' except by the Holy Spirit." -1 Cor. 12:3.

Harvest admitted, "I thought since Vessel testified to me, who He Is, *he* was the one who led me to Jesus."

Vessel laughed sheepishly, "I am grateful I was given the opportunity to share the testimony of who He Is with you. To water the seed of God's word, which your Vacation Bible School teacher sowed in you, yet all the glory of Salvation goes to Him and His goodness."

"It is the goodness of God that leads us to repentance." Surv explained. "Vessel testified to you of who He Is, yet it is the Treasure of goodness He Is that led all of us to Him."

"As Vessel testified to you, Holy Spirit was right there with you and him, hovering as watchman over the voice of the testimony of who He Is, just as He hovered over the face of the water in the very beginning.

The Bible introduced us to His Spirit by saying,

> The earth was without form, and void, and darkness was on the face of the deep. And the Spirit of God was hovering over the face of the waters.
> —Gen. 1:2

Fire

Holiness

AT sunset, the families all gathered together on the dock to watch as golden glimmers of light reflected off the water.

"Makes you want to dive right in, doesn't it?" asked Harvest.

Feeling the cool in the air, Vessel responded, "That water is cold!"

Without looking away from the water, Harvest responded, "I was referring to diving into the testimony of who He Is, to be completely immersed in all that He Is."

Surv leaned forward, "Harvest, that's a really good example of how Jesus baptizes us when we receive Him as Lord over our life, John the Baptist said:

> I indeed baptize you with water unto repentance, but He who is coming after me is mightier than I, whose sandals I am not worthy to carry. He will baptize you with the Holy Spirit and fire.
>
> —Matt. 3:11

John the Baptist immersed followers of God with natural water, as testimony of the person giving of oneself unto repentance to God."

"Jesus baptizes, by immersing His people with the Holy Spirit, sealing us with the promise that He has given Himself for us."

"And He immerses us with fire to purify us for His holy purpose.

> Or do you not know that your body is the temple
> of the Holy Spirit who is in you, whom you have
> from God, and you are not your own?
> —1 Cor. 6:19

Vessel grinning from ear to ear raised his hands and declared, "See, I told you I'm a treasure chest and the Treasure He Is lives within me!"

Surv chuckled, "Yes Vessel, all who believe in Jesus are as you say 'a treasure chest.' Our bodies are the temple of the Holy Spirit; therefore our body is sanctified for the Treasure of holiness He Is."

Cloud

Gentle Kindness

BY this time, Vessel and the children were bringing light to the darkness as they swarmed around the bank of the river with the light of fiery sparklers.

As the adults carefully watched over the children, Harvest asked, "I heard the pastor say Holy Spirit is gentle as a dove. How do we know He is present if He is so gentle?"

From a distance, where he was swirling a sparkler like a child, Vessel jumped in, "We know because when the Holy Spirit comes upon us, heaven speaks!"

"Yes" agreed Surv. "Like when Jesus was baptized by John the Baptist the scripture says;

> When He had been baptized, Jesus came up immediately from the water; and behold, the heavens were opened to Him, and He saw the Spirit of God descending like a dove and alighting upon Him. And suddenly a voice came from heaven, saying, "This is My beloved Son, in whom I am well pleased."
>
> —Matt. 3:16–17

As soon as Jesus came up from the water the Holy Spirit descended upon Him and the voice of the Father came from heaven and formally introduced His Son Jesus."

"And the day the Holy Spirit was sent to earth to be our Helper, Scripture tells us a sound came down from heaven filling the whole house where the disciples were gathered, and they all were filled with the Holy Spirit. And when they were filled with the Holy Spirit, a sound came out of them! The disciple's voices became the sound! They all began to speak in different languages, languages they didn't even know!"

"Yes!" Vessel eagerly jumped in again. "But there were several people listening nearby, people from nations all over the world. They knew the languages, and they understood the words of the disciples because the disciples were speaking *their* native languages. And those people who knew the languages testified that the disciples were declaring the wonderful works of God!"

Surv explained, "When the Holy Spirit came upon them, the disciples received the Treasure of gentle kindness He Is, making them witnesses to the testimony of who He Is for the nations of the world to hear! Jesus said:

> He who believes in Me, as the Scripture has said,
> out of his heart will flow rivers of living water.
> —John 7:38

And that is exactly what happened when the disciples received the Holy Spirit. He was the source of their words.

Therefore, their voice of testimony had become alive, it had become living water!"

"It is the same when the witness of the Holy Spirit comes upon us; He fills us with words of His testimony. That we might be His gentle and kind witnesses to the world; that we might testify of the wonderful works of God."

Living Water

Life

THE light of the moon gently lit the faces of the families as they gathered together to say their good-bye's with prayer and thanksgiving.

Eager to express His thankfulness, Harvest said, "I am grateful for all of you. You have all been so kind in sharing the testimony of who He Is with me. It is because you allowed Him to use you, His temple for His holy purpose, that I now understand the true reason we celebrate the Treasure of the Christmas season. Most of all, I am thankful the Treasure of who He Is lives in me. So thankful I wish I could tell it to the world!"

Vessel laughed and said, "Harvest, you know the first men Jesus called to preach the gospel were fishermen."

"Preach!" shrieked Harvest. "I didn't mean I would literally tell the world. I'm not a preacher."

Surv shook his head at Vessel and smiled. "Not to worry, Harvest, 'preach the gospel' simply means to proclaim the good news of who He Is to the world, to gently drop words like rain by kindly sharing the testimony of who He Is with others. Just as Jesus called His disciples, He has called us:

And He said to them, "Go into all the world and preach the gospel to every creature."

—Mark 16:15

With humility, Harvest replied, "Well, since that's what it means to preach, then I'm honored our Lord chose this ol' fisherman to testify of who He Is."

Vessel added, "As His temple we are to be a resemblance of the temple the prophet Ezekiel saw in a prophetic vision."

"Yes," Surv agreed, "Ezekiel saw the temple of God filled with the glory of the Lord. Flowing from the threshold of the temple was water. As the shallow water flowed from the temple, it became deeper and deeper, until it was a healing river of life."

"When we testify of the Treasure of life He Is, our voice flows as deep healing waters throughout the world that all who hear might come and freely drink from His healing river of life."

The families joined hands as Vessel ended the night with prayer. "Father, You are good and Your mercy endures forever. We commit ourselves to the call of Your holy purpose, surrendering ourselves to You that our voices might be a reflection of the gentle kindness of Your Holy Spirit."

"Therefore, we will not wait on the angels of heaven to stir the water, nor will we wait on the wind or the rain. But according to your holy purpose, we will lift up our voices with the testimony of who You are. And we will let the rivers of living water flow!"

"In Jesus name, we pray, Your kingdom come, Your will be done on earth as it is in heaven. Amen."

As the families all said their good-byes and began to walk away, the children sang: "Don't Look for the Wind! Don't Look for the Rain! Because Here I Come! Calling His Name!"

"And He said to them, "Go into all the world and preach the gospel to every creature."

—Mark 16:15

Additional Scripture Study

Chapter 1 - Hope

"But we have this treasure in earthen vessels that the excellence of the power may be of God and not of us" (2 Cor. 4:7).

"This is hope we have as an anchor of the soul, both sure and steadfast, and which enters the Presence behind the veil" (Heb. 6:19).

"The Lord is not slack concerning His promise, as some count slackness; but is longsuffering toward us, not willing that any should perish but that all should come to repentance" (2 Peter 3:9).

"Now may the God of hope fill you with all joy and peace in believing, that you may abound in hope by the power of the Holy Spirit" (Rom. 15:13).

Chapter 2 - Faith

"For God did not send His Son into the world to condemn the world, but that the world through Him might be saved" (John 3:17).

"But the hour is coming, and now is, when the true worshipers will worship the Father in spirit and truth; for the Father is seeking such to worship Him"(John 4:23).

"So then faith comes by hearing, and hearing by the word of God" (Rom. 10:17).

"I have been crucified with Christ; it is no longer I who live, but Christ lives in me; and the life which I now live in the flesh I live by faith in the Son of God, who loved me and gave Himself for me" (Gal. 2:20).

Chapter 3 - Peace

"Therefore pray the Lord of the harvest to send out laborers into His Harvest" (Matt. 9:38).

"Do you not say, 'There are still four months and then comes the harvest?' Behold, I say to you, lift up your eyes and look at the fields, for they are already white for harvest'" (John 4:35).

"Jesus said to him, "I am the way, the truth, and the life. No one comes to the Father except through Me" (John 14:6).

"No more shall every man teach his neighbor, and every man his brother, saying, "Know the LORD for they all shall know Me, from the least of them to the greatest of them, says the LORD. For I will forgive their iniquity, and their sin I will remember no more" (Jer. 31:34).

Chapter 4 - Joy

"Again, the kingdom of heaven is like treasure hidden in a field, which a man found and hid; and for joy over it he goes and sells all that he has and buys that field" (Matt. 13:44).

"I rejoice at Your word as one who finds great treasure" (Ps. 119:162).

"For it is the God who commanded light to shine out of darkness, who has shone in our hearts to give the light of the knowledge of the glory of God in the face of Jesus Christ" (2 Cor. 4:6).

"For where your treasure is, there your heart will be also" (Luke 12:34).

Chapter 5 - Righteousness

"How much more shall the blood of Christ, who through the eternal Spirit offered Himself without spot to God, cleanse your conscience from dead works to serve the living God?" (Heb. 9–14).

"For He made Him who knew no sin to be sin for us, that we might become the righteousness of God in Him" (2 Cor. 5:21).

"Give us this day our daily bread" (Matt. 6-11).

Chapter 6 - Blessing

"And whatever you ask in My name, that I will do that the Father may be glorified in the Son" (John 14:13).

"And the LORD, He is the One who goes before you. He will be with you. He will not leave you nor forsake you; do not fear or be dismayed" (Deut. 31:8).

"Christ has redeemed us from the curse of the law, having become a curse for us (for it is written, *'Cursed is everyone who hangs on a tree.'*)" (Gal. 3:13).

Chapter 7 - Grace

"Be angry, and do not sin" do not let the sun go down on your wrath," (Eph. 4:26).

"For we do not have a High Priest who cannot sympathize with our weaknesses, but was in all points tempted as we are, yet without sin" (Heb. 4:15).

"But He gives more grace. Therefore He says: 'God resists the proud, but gives grace to the humble'" (James 4:6).

Chapter 8 - Mercy

"After this, Jesus, knowing that all things were now accomplished, that the Scripture might be fulfilled said, 'I thirst'" (John 19:28).

"And Jesus said to them, 'I am the bread of life. He who comes to Me shall never hunger, and he who believes in Me shall never thirst'" (John 6:35).

"Let us therefore come boldly to the throne of grace, that we may obtain mercy and find grace to help in time of need"(Heb. 4:16).

"Jesus said to them, "Come and eat breakfast." Yet none of the disciples dared ask Him. "Who are You?" – knowing that it was the Lord." Jesus then came and took the bread and gave it to them, and likewise the fish" (John 21:12-13).

Chapter 9 – Rest

"Then God blessed the seventh day and sanctified it, because in it He rested from all His work which God had created and made."(Gen. 2:3).

"Therefore, since a promise remains of entering His rest, let us fear lest any of you seem to have come short of it."(Heb. 4:1)

Chapter 10 - Knowledge

"For the earth will be filled with the knowledge of the glory of the LORD as the waters cover the sea" (Hab. 2:14).

"I set My rainbow in the cloud, and it shall be for the sign of the covenant between Me and the earth" (Gen. 9:13).

"In whom are hidden all the treasures of wisdom and knowledge" (Col 2.3)

Chapter 11 - Truth

"The Lord will guide you continually and satisfy your soul in drought, and strengthen your bones; you shall be like a watered garden, and like a spring of water, whose waters do not fail" (Isa. 58:11).

"The earth was without form, and void, and darkness was on the face of the deep. And the Spirit of God was hovering over the face of the waters" (Gen. 1:2).

"For we walk by faith, not by sight."(2 Cor. 5:7).

"Jesus said to him, 'I am the way, the truth, and the life. No one comes to the Father except through Me'" (John 14:6).

Chapter 12 – Victory

"I will give you a new heart and put a new spirit within you; I will take the heart of stone out of your flesh and give you a heart of flesh" (Ezek. 36:26).

"For from within, out of the heart of men, proceed evil thoughts, adulteries, fornications, murders, thefts, covetousness, wickedness, deceit, lewdness, an evil eye, blasphemy, pride, foolishness"(Mark 7:21-22).

"For whatever is born of God overcomes the world. And this is the victory that has overcome the world – our faith" (1 John 5:4).

"Therefore if the Son makes you free, you shall be free indeed" (John 8:36).

Chapter 13 - Love

"For even the Son of Man, did not come to be served, but to serve, and to give His life a ransom for many" (Mark 10:45).

"And He said to them, 'This is My blood of the new covenant, which is shed for many" (Mark 14: 24).

"Love does no harm to a neighbor; therefore love is the fulfillment of the law" (Rom. 13:10).

"That at the name of Jesus every knee should bow, of those in heaven, and of those on earth, and of those under the earth and that every tongue should confess that Jesus Christ is Lord, to the glory of God the Father" (Phil 2:10-11).

Chapter 14 - Goodness

"The Spirit of truth, whom the world cannot receive, because it neither sees Him nor knows Him; but you know Him, for He dwells with you and will be in you" (John 14:17).

"No one can come to Me unless the Father who sent Me draws him; and I will raise him up at the last day" (John 6:44).

"Nevertheless I tell you the truth. It is to your advantage that I go away; for if I do not go away, the Helper will not come to you; but if I depart, I will send Him to you. And when He has come, He will convict the world of sin, and of righteousness, and of judgment" (John 16:7–8).

"Or do you despise the riches of His goodness, forbearance, and longsuffering, not knowing that the goodness of God leads you to repentance" (Rom. 2:4).

Chapter 15 - Holiness

"In Him you also trusted, after you heard the word of truth, the gospel of your salvation; in whom also, having believed, you were sealed with the Holy Spirit of promise" (Eph. 1:13).

"Who has saved us and called us with a holy calling, not according to our works, but according to His own purpose and grace which was given to us in Christ Jesus before time began" (2 Tim. 1:9).

"But we have this treasure in earthen vessels, that the excellence of the power may be of God and not of us" (2 Cor. 4:7).

Chapter 16 – Gentle Kindness

"And behold, the glory of the God of Israel came from the way of the east. His voice was like the sound of many waters; and the earth shone with His glory" (Ezek. 43:2).

"And suddenly there came a sound from heaven, as of a rushing mighty wind, and it filled the whole house where they were sitting" (Acts 2:2).

"But you shall receive power when the Holy Spirit has come upon you; and you shall be witnesses to Me in Jerusalem, and in all Judea and Samaria, and to the end of the earth" (Acts 1:8).

Chapter 17 – Life

"Then Jesus said to them, 'Follow Me, and I will make you become fishers of men'" (Mark 1:17).

"Let my teaching drop as the rain, my speech distill as dew, as raindrops on the tender herb, and as showers on the grass "(Deut. 32:2).

"And it shall be that every living thing that moves, wherever the rivers go, will live. There will be a very great multitude of fish, because these waters go there; for they will be healed, and everything will live wherever the river goes" (Ezek. 47:9).

"Nor will they say, "See here!' or 'See there!' For indeed, the kingdom of God is within you" (Luke 17:21).

About the Author

SUSIE Michaels diligently searched the Holy Scriptures for five years before she discovered the answer to the riddle of water: what is the significance of water in the Bible, and why did Jesus turn it into wine? Water is mentioned over 600 times in the Bible, not including rain, wells, rivers, the sea, springs, and brooks. Surely water, the water Jesus turned into wine, has significant purpose, a purpose our heavenly Father intended for us to draw upon and the Treasure He desires us to seek. The Treasure led Susie to write Watering Harvest.

Watering Harvest Mission Statement:
We will water the world with the Good News of Jesus Christ because He asked us to.

"Go therefore and make disciples of all the nations, baptizing them in the name of the Father and of the Son and of the Holy Spirit, teaching them to observe all things that I have commanded you, and lo I am with you always, even to the end of the age. Amen." - Matthew 28:19-20

Connect with Watering Harvest
Visit us on the web www.wateringharvest.com
Like us on Facebook
Follow us on Twitter